MW01201949

DUE DATE

NOV 0 3

Let Freedom Ring

The Massachusetts 54th:
African American Soldiers of the Union

by Gina DeAngelis

Consultant:
Stephen E. Osman
Historic Fort Snelling
St. Paul, Minnesota

Bridgestone Books
an imprint of Capstone Press
Mankato, Minnesota

Bridgestone Books are published by Capstone Press
151 Good Counsel Drive, P.O. Box 669, Mankato, Minnesota 56002
http://www.capstone-press.com

Library of Congress Cataloging-in-Publication Data
DeAngelis, Gina
    The Massachusetts 54th: African American soldiers of the Union/by Gina DeAngelis.
        p. cm.—(Let freedom ring)
    Summary: Explains the events leading up to the formation of the Massachusetts 54th,
a regiment of free blacks, and its participation in the Civil War. Sidebars include
quotations from leaders of the time and facts about African American soldiers.
Includes bibliographical references and index.
    ISBN 0-7368-1343-8 (hardcover)
    1. United States. Army. Massachusetts Infantry Regiment, 54th (1863–1865)—
Juvenile literature. 2. United States—History—Civil War, 1861–1865—Participation,
African American—Juvenile literature. 3. African American soldiers—History—19th
century—Juvenile literature. 4. Massachusetts—History—Civil War, 1861–1865—
Regimental histories—Juvenile literature. 5. United States—History—Civil War,
1861–1865—Regimental histories—Juvenile literature. [1. United States. Army.
Massachusetts Infantry Regiment, 54th (1863–1865). 2. United States—History—
Civil War, 1861–1865—Participation, African American. 3. African American
soldiers—History—19th century.] I. Title: Massachusetts Fifty-fourth. II. Title.
III. Series.
E513.5 54th .D43 2003
973.7'444—dc21   2001008435

Editorial Credits

Blake A. Hoena, editor; Kia Adams, series designer; Juliette Peters, book designer;
Erin Scott/SARIN Creative, illustrator; Kelly Garvin, photo researcher; Karen Risch,
product planning editor

Photo Credits

Bettmann/Corbis, cover; Naval Historic Foundation, 5; Stock Montage, Inc., 6, 13, 17;
Corbis, 8, 42, 43; North Wind Picture Archives, 10, 14, 18, 20, 24, 32, 35, 41; National
Archives, 15; Florida State Archives, 23, 38; Library of Congress, 26, 31; South Carolina
Historical Society, 28–29, Kurt Jacoboni, Lakeland MI, 37

1   2   3   4   5   6   07   06   05   04   03   02

Table of Contents

Chapter One

The Civil War

Robert Smalls worked as a slave aboard the steamship *Planter*. He piloted this ship along South Carolina's coast during the Civil War (1861–1865). The Confederate Navy used *Planter* to carry supplies.

On May 12, 1862, the *Planter* was docked at Charleston, South Carolina. The ship's captain and other white crewmembers left to attend a party that night. They left Smalls and the other slaves alone aboard the ship.

Smalls had planned for just this moment. The slaves' families had hidden nearby. They boarded the ship after the white crewmembers left. Smalls then piloted *Planter* past the Confederate forts guarding Charleston Harbor. Once he reached safety, Smalls surrendered the ship and its cargo to the Union.

People in the North considered Smalls a hero for his actions. Smalls then joined the fight against the Confederacy as a Union officer aboard the *Planter*.

During the Civil War, Confederates used the *Planter* as a supply ship.

Frederick Douglass

Frederick Augustus Washington Bailey was born a slave in Maryland around 1818. He ran away when he was 20 years old. He then changed his name to Frederick Douglass to keep from being recognized as an escaped slave.

In 1845, Douglass wrote his autobiography. This book was about his life as a slave. He founded the antislavery newspaper *North Star* in 1847. Douglass often spoke out against slavery.

Douglass became a famous speaker and abolitionist. He often discussed his views on slavery with President Abraham Lincoln.

During the Civil War, almost 200,000 African Americans joined the Union military. Many joined because they believed that they were fighting for their freedom. Among African American regiments, the 54th Massachusetts Volunteer Infantry Regiment was one of the first and most well known.

Issues That Led to War

The disagreement on states' rights was the main issue that led to the Civil War. Most Northerners believed in a strong central government, which would make laws for all states. Southerners believed that each state had the right to make its own laws.

The North had a larger population than the South. This difference made Southerners worry that a strong central government would be controlled by Northerners. Southerners feared that Northerners would pass national laws, such as making slavery illegal, that would hurt their way of life. The South's economy was based on growing crops on large farms called plantations. Southerners used slaves to work these farms. The North's economy was based on producing factory goods. Slaves were not needed for factory work. Slavery was actually illegal in Northern states.

During the early 1800s, many Americans were beginning to move west into frontier lands. As these new lands filled with people, new states were formed. Lawmakers in the North and South argued whether slavery should be legal in these new states. Slave states and free, or nonslave, states often voted against each other on important issues in Congress. The North did not want any new slave states voting on issues in Congress. Southerners did not want free states passing laws that would harm their way of life.

Secession and War

Abraham Lincoln was a candidate for president in the election of 1860. Lincoln had promised not to end slavery where it existed. But he also said that he did not want slavery to spread into new states.

Lincoln won the election even though few Southerners voted for him. But Southerners feared that Lincoln would break his promise and make slavery illegal. Eleven states decided to secede, or

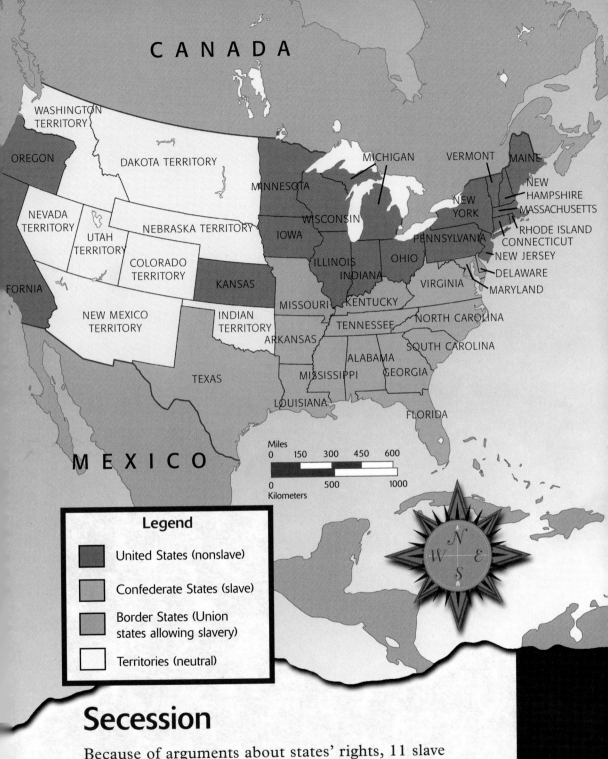

CANADA

WASHINGTON
TERRITORY

OREGON

DAKOTA TERRITORY

MICHIGAN   VERMONT   MAINE

MINNESOTA   NEW
                                       HAMPSHIRE
NEVADA   WISCONSIN   NEW   MASSACHUSETTS
TERRITORY   NEBRASKA TERRITORY IOWA   YORK
       UTAH   RHODE ISLAND
       TERRITORY   PENNSYLVANIA CONNECTICUT
                 COLORADO   ILLINOIS OHIO   NEW JERSEY
FORNIA   TERRITORY   INDIANA   DELAWARE
                        KANSAS   VIRGINIA   MARYLAND
            NEW MEXICO   MISSOURI KENTUCKY
            TERRITORY   INDIAN   NORTH CAROLINA
                        TERRITORY TENNESSEE
                        ARKANSAS   SOUTH CAROLINA
              TEXAS   ALABAMA   GEORGIA
                        MISSISSIPPI
                    LOUISIANA   FLORIDA

MEXICO

Miles
0   150   300   450   600

0   500   1000
Kilometers

Legend

- United States (nonslave)
- Confederate States (slave)
- Border States (Union states allowing slavery)
- Territories (neutral)

Secession

Because of arguments about states' rights, 11 slave states seceded from the United States and formed the Confederate States of America, or the Confederacy.

withdraw, from the United States. They formed their own nation, the Confederate States of America, also called the Confederacy. This action led to the Civil War.

The Treatment of African Americans

As slaves, African American men, women, and children were considered property. Whites bought and sold them much like cattle. The law allowed slave owners to whip and even starve their slaves.

At the beginning of the Civil War, African Americans were not allowed to fight in either the Union Army or the Confederate Army. But both armies used them as laborers.

Many slaves tried to escape these conditions. They ran away to the North where slavery was illegal. But even in the North, African Americans were not treated well. Although they were not whipped, free African Americans could not vote or serve on juries. In many places, African Americans could not sit with whites in public places. They were not allowed to go into many restaurants, hotels, and schools. They had a hard time finding good jobs. Frederick Douglass, a skilled shipbuilder, had to dig cellars and collect trash to earn a living. Like Douglass, most free African Americans worked at low-paying jobs.

African American men and women worked for both the Confederate Army and the Union Army during the war. Men drove wagons, dug graves, or worked as laborers. Women washed laundry or cooked. But at the beginning of the war, African American men were not allowed to join the army. They were told that the war was a white man's fight.

Chapter Two

Focus of the War

At first, most Northerners and Southerners declared that the Civil War was not about slavery. Northerners said the war was being fought to preserve the Union. Southerners said the war was fought to preserve their way of life.

Abolitionists and African Americans disagreed. They believed the main issue behind the war was slavery. In 1861, Frederick Douglass said, "There is nothing existing between [North and South] to prevent peace but . . . slavery. Everybody knows this, everybody feels this, and yet the great mass of the people refuse to confess it, and the government refuses to recognize it."

Freed Slaves

Union generals dealt in different ways with slaves freed during the war. In the summer of 1861, General John Frémont freed slaves in Missouri and Kansas. He then enlisted them in the Union Army. Union leaders did not approve of these actions, and Lincoln removed Frémont from his command.

John Frémont was a famous American explorer of the West. During the Civil War, he was removed from his command for enlisting African Americans in the Union Army.

Another Union general, Benjamin Butler, declared that slaves behind enemy lines were contraband. Contraband is illegal goods, such as ammunition and guns, which help an enemy fight a war. Butler refused to return slaves to their Southern owners because slaves helped the Confederacy fight the war. The South used slaves to dig ditches and guard camps or forts.

Lincoln wanted to wait until a Union victory to announce the Emancipation Proclamation. This victory came at the Battle of Antietam in 1862.

Butler's term became popular. During the Civil War, the word "contraband" applied to African Americans who had been freed by, or who ran away to, the Union Army.

Steps toward Freedom

In July 1862, Congress passed the Confiscation Act. This law authorized President Lincoln to allow African Americans to join the Union Army as soldiers. Congress also repealed, or took back, a law passed in 1792 that kept African Americans from serving in the military.

Also in 1862, Lincoln decided that slavery must end. After the Union victory at the Battle of Antietam, Maryland, in September, Lincoln issued the Emancipation Proclamation. This order declared that as of January 1, 1863, all slaves in Confederate states were free.

Lincoln's proclamation did not free slaves in slave states that stayed in the Union. But the Emancipation Proclamation turned the war into a fight to end slavery. Abolitionists were overjoyed.

Chapter Three

The 54th
Is Formed

In January 1863, Governor John Andrew of Massachusetts received permission to form a regiment of African American soldiers. Andrew then asked a well-known abolitionist named Francis Shaw if his son, Robert Gould Shaw, would command the 54th Massachusetts Volunteer Infantry Regiment.

At the time, Robert Shaw was a captain in the 2nd Massachusetts Volunteer Infantry Regiment. He knew that an African American regiment would not be very popular, even in the North. He also knew many whites believed that African American troops would fail in battle, and their failure would be blamed on their race. But these drawbacks did not stop Shaw. He agreed to lead the 54th Massachusetts.

In 1863, the U.S. government began to allow African Americans to enlist in the army.

Robert Gould Shaw

Robert Shaw was educated in New York and Europe and attended Harvard College in Massachusetts. He joined the 7th New York militia even before the Civil War began. In May 1861, he became an officer in the 2nd Massachusetts Volunteer Infantry. When he agreed to lead the 54th Massachusetts, Shaw was only 25 years old.

Robert Shaw commanded the 54th Massachusetts until his death. As commander of the regiment, he was commissioned as a colonel.

Recruiting for the 54th

Frederick Douglass, as well as other abolitionist leaders, gave speeches urging African Americans to enlist in the army. To encourage people to join the 54th, Douglass said, "Liberty won by white men would lack half its luster. Who would be free themselves must strike the blow." Some of the 54th's first members were sons of Douglass, Lewis and Charles.

The African American population in Massachusetts was small, so recruiting for the 54th took place across the North. People volunteered from New York, Pennsylvania, Michigan, Ohio, Vermont, and New Jersey. Some escaped slaves from the South even joined the regiment.

Colonel Shaw was strict about the men he allowed to enlist. He accepted only the healthiest and strongest men into the regiment. Many of the recruits were also better educated than average African Americans. Shaw hoped that these high standards would help the regiment succeed.

By the end of April, the regiment was full. So many men had volunteered to join the 54th that a second regiment, the 55th Massachusetts, was formed.

Camp Life

The volunteers went to Camp Meigs in Readville, Massachusetts. There, they were formed into companies, or groups of 100, and given uniforms and weapons. The companies spent their days

The 55th Massachusetts was created because so many African Americans wanted to enlist in the 54th. In 1865, the 55th helped liberate Charleston, South Carolina.

Did You Know?

White and African American soldiers in the U.S. armed forces did not live and work together from 1792 until 1948, when President Harry Truman issued Executive Order 9981. This document set up the President's Committee on Equality of Treatment and Opportunity in the military. The committee helped ensure that all U.S. soldiers were treated equally.

training and adjusting to army life. Because they were African American, they lived separately from the white troops who trained at the camp.

Many people, especially African Americans, were eager to see these new troops. The soldiers also were anxious to show off what they had learned. On May 28, 1863, the 54th marched through the streets of Boston to the cheers of its citizens. The 54th's members then boarded the steamship *De Molay*, which carried them to Hilton Head, South Carolina.

Chapter Four

First Action

Union General David Hunter supported African American troops. Early in 1862, Hunter formed a regiment with slaves that he had freed in South Carolina. In November 1862, Union Army leaders recognized Hunter's unit, the 1st South Carolina Volunteers. It became the first African American unit in the Union Army.

General Hunter's troops and the 54th Massachusetts belonged to the Department of the South. These Union troops dug trenches and built roads for the Union Army. They sometimes went on expeditions into Confederate territory to attack enemy targets.

In 1863, Union generals decided to attack Charleston, South Carolina, an important Confederate port. Taking Charleston would be a great victory for the North. Fort Sumter, which protected Charleston Harbor, was where the Civil War began. But many other forts also guarded the area.

Members of the 54th Massachusetts were part of the Union's Department of the South.

General Quincy Gillmore planned the attack on Charleston. Several forts guarded Charleston Harbor. These forts included Fort Moultrie on Sullivans Island, Fort Johnson on James Island, and Fort Wagner on Morris Island. Gillmore wanted to attack Fort Wagner first.

Fort Moultrie was one of the forts defending Charleston from attack by sea. This image is from before the Civil War began.

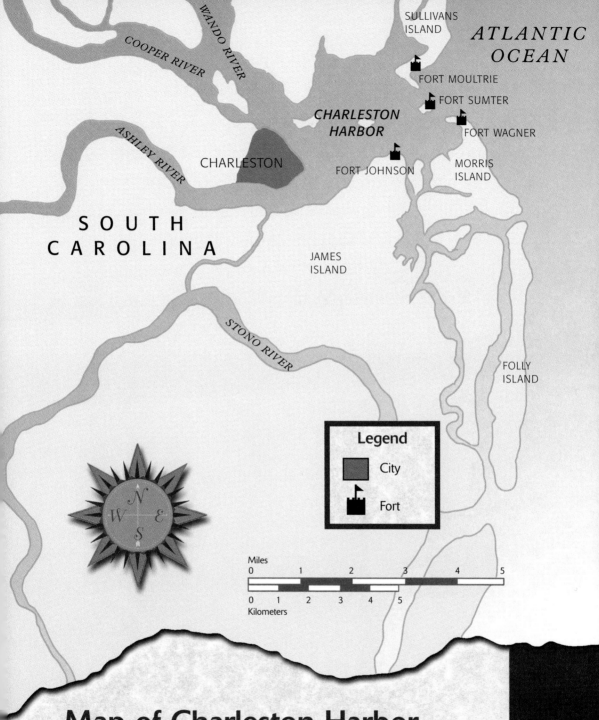

Map of Charleston Harbor

Several forts protected Charleston from attack by sea.

Fort Wagner

Fort Wagner was very well protected. It was
surrounded on three sides by water and swamp.
The only approach to the fort by land was a
.5-mile (.8-kilometer) long, narrow strip of beach,
which ended at a moat of waist-deep water. The
walls of the fort, built of sand and logs, were about
25 feet (7.6 meters) high.

General Quincy
Gillmore led several
attacks against
Charleston and the forts
surrounding its harbor.

The Union Army first attacked Fort Wagner on July 10. General Gillmore's troops attacked without success. More than 300 men were killed or wounded during the fighting.

Gillmore planned a larger attack for July 18. The Union Navy would bombard the fort from the sea to weaken Fort Wagner's walls. Under cover of night, Union troops would then approach the fort by land.

The 54th

During the initial fighting on Morris Island, the 54th was on James Island. On July 16, three companies of the regiment were on picket, or guard, duty when a force of about 4,000 Confederates attacked. The men of the 54th fought bravely, and with the help of other Union regiments, drove the Confederates back.

After the fighting, Shaw received orders for his troops to report to General George Strong on Morris Island. Strong would direct the troops attacking Fort Wagner.

The 54th had some trouble getting to Morris Island. The soldiers marched for hours, through swamps and in pouring rain, to cross James Island. Then a ship carried them to Folly Island. But there was no place for the ship to dock, and there was only one small boat to take troops to the ship. It took all night to get the entire regiment on board.

The men arrived on Folly Island having had no sleep or food since the previous day. They then

marched 6 miles (9.7 kilometers) to another ship. This ship carried them to Morris Island. They arrived at about 6:00 at night on July 18.

General Strong told Shaw that the 54th could lead the attack on Fort Wagner. Despite their hunger and exhaustion, the men of the 54th saw this act as a great honor. They also saw it as an opportunity to prove themselves in combat.

Confederate soldiers at Fort Wagner built bombproof shelters to hide in when the Union Navy fired its cannons at the fort.

Chapter Five

Fort Wagner

Just before sunset on July 18, 1863, the tired and hungry men of the 54th assembled on Morris Island's beach. They stood about 1 mile (1.6 kilometers) from Fort Wagner.

At 7:45 at night, Colonel Shaw ordered his men to march toward the fort. On their right was the Atlantic Ocean. On their left was swamp. A few hundred yards (meters) from the fort, the beach narrowed to 100 feet (30 meters) across. The Confederates could easily aim their cannons and rifles at the 54th's members marching through this area. The men moved forward despite the hail of enemy fire.

The Battle

When the 54th reached the fort's walls, the soldiers flung themselves at the enemy. They fought with rifle butts and bayonets. Civil War soldiers attached these metal blades to the end of their rifles.

Seeing African Americans in uniform changed many Northerners' impression. An African American in uniform with a rifle seemed deserving of respect.

The soldiers of the 54th fought bravely during the Battle of Fort Wagner, but Union forces were never able to capture the fort.

Brave Moments

Captain Luis Emilio of the 54th wrote about Shaw's bravery during the battle, "He stood there for a moment with uplifted sword, shouting 'Forward, Fifty-Fourth!' and then fell dead, shot through the heart, besides other wounds."

A soldier in the 54th named James Henry Gooding recalled, "Colonel Shaw seized the staff [of the Massachusetts flag] when the [flag] bearer fell, and in less than a minute after, the Colonel fell himself."

About 1,700 Confederate troops were in the fort. Only a few dozen members of the 54th reached the fort's walls. They fought bravely, but not enough of them remained to continue the fight for long.

Reinforcements also did not arrive in time to help the 54th. Soldiers could not march across the narrow strip of beach to reach the 54th quickly enough. The 54th suffered heavy losses during the battle. Of the 600 members of the 54th involved in the fighting, 256 were either killed, wounded, or missing by battle's end. Colonel Shaw also was killed.

Prisoners of War

The Confederate government opposed the use of African Americans as soldiers. In December 1862, it declared that African Americans captured in a Union uniform would be sent into slavery. In May 1863, the Confederate government proclaimed that any white officer commanding African American troops would be executed.

To counter Confederate threats, President Lincoln issued a proclamation on July 30, 1863. He stated, "For every soldier of the United States killed in violation of the laws of war, a Rebel soldier shall be executed, and for every one enslaved by the enemy or sold into slavery, a Rebel soldier shall be placed at hard labor on the public works." The Confederacy did not execute or send into slavery any prisoners from the 54th Massachusetts.

Union forces were never able to capture Fort Wagner. But later, the Confederates abandoned it.

After the Battle

Even though the attack on July 18 failed, it was a great success in one sense. The soldiers of the 54th Massachusetts proved that African Americans were brave soldiers. They fought hard and won the respect of many whites.

Thousands of African American men were eager to join the now-famous 54th. More states formed African American regiments, and more white soldiers were willing to fight alongside them.

More African Americans were eager to join the Union Army after they heard news of the 54th's bravery.

Chapter Six

Remembering the 54th

Governor John Andrew had promised the soldiers of the 54th Massachusetts equal pay. White soldiers were paid $13 a month, plus $3 dollars for clothing. But when payday came, the soldiers of the 54th were offered only $10, minus $3 for clothing.

The 54th's members refused to accept any pay unless it was equal to white soldiers' pay. Their decision caused hardship for their families. Their families often did not have enough money for food. But to the soldiers it was not an issue of money, rather one of pride. Even when Governor Andrew offered to make up the difference from the Massachusetts state treasury, the 54th's members refused. They wanted the U.S. government to pay them the wages that they deserved.

Battle of Olustee

As the war continued, Union forces moved farther south. In January 1864, the

African American soldiers did not receive pay equal to white soldiers' until the war was almost over. This one dollar bill is an example of U.S. currency during the Civil War.

54th was sent to Florida under General Truman Seymour's command.

On February 20, Seymour led his troops into an ill-fated battle at the Olustee train station. Nearly 2,000 Union soldiers were killed, wounded, or missing during the battle. The Union Army also lost a great deal of supplies and equipment during the fighting.

The 54th did not take part in the main battle. They were about 3 miles (5 kilometers) from the fighting. But when Seymour realized his army had lost the battle, he ordered the 54th to protect the

The 54th is best known for the Battle of Fort Wagner, but it also fought in the Battle of Olustee.

Did You Know?

African Americans made up 4 to 5 percent of the North's population during the Civil War. But African American soldiers made up 10 to 12 percent of the Union Army by the end of the war.

army's retreat. The 54th prevented Confederate soldiers from following Seymour's troops and allowed them to escape.

After the battle was over, the members of the 54th learned about a broken-down train carrying wounded. The members of the 54th used ropes to pull the train several miles (kilometers) to safety.

The 54th lost 87 out of 500 men who fought during the battle. In April 1864, the 54th returned to South Carolina.

Remembering African American Soldiers

The 54th was not the first African American regiment in the Union Army. But it was the first raised in the North. It helped pave the way for many more African American units. About

Equal Pay

In June 1864, Congress gave equal pay to African Americans in the Union Army. However, the law required that African American soldiers had to have been free as of April 19, 1861, the day the Civil War began, to receive this pay.

Many African Americans still were unhappy about their pay. It was not until March 1865, a month before the war ended, that Congress finally agreed to pay former slaves in the army the same amount as white soldiers.

179,000 African Americans would serve in the Union Army during the Civil War. Another 19,000 served in the Union Navy.

Today, the site where Fort Wagner stood has been washed away by ocean tides. But the sacrifice made by the 54th Massachusetts is remembered within the Fort Sumter National Monument.

In 1897, a monument in Boston Common was dedicated to Robert Shaw and the 54th Massachusetts. Artist Augustus Saint-Gaudens sculpted the monument. It shows Shaw on horseback surrounded by African American troops.

On July 18, 1998, the African American Civil War Memorial was dedicated in Washington, D.C. A statue, sculpted by artist Ed Hamilton, portrays African American soldiers and sailors who served during the war. The memorial's Wall of Honor bears the names of more than 209,000 African American soldiers and their officers.

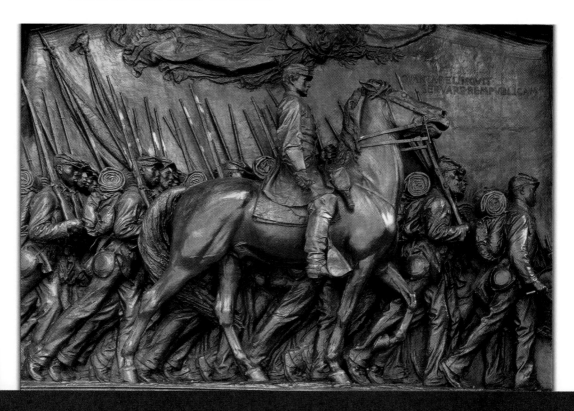

Artist Augustus Saint-Gaudens created this statue of Robert Shaw and the 54th. It can be seen in Boston Common in Boston.

TIMELINE

February to June: 10 Southern states join South Carolina to form the Confederate States of America.

September: The Battle of Antietam is fought.

November: Abraham Lincoln is elected president of the United States.

July: Congress passes the Conscription Act, which repeals a law forbidding African Americans from serving in the military.

1860   **1861**   **1862**

December: South Carolina secedes from the Union.

April: The Civil War begins when Southerners fire on Fort Sumter, South Carolina.

November: The 1st South Carolina, a regiment of form[er] slaves, is recognized by the U.S. War Department.

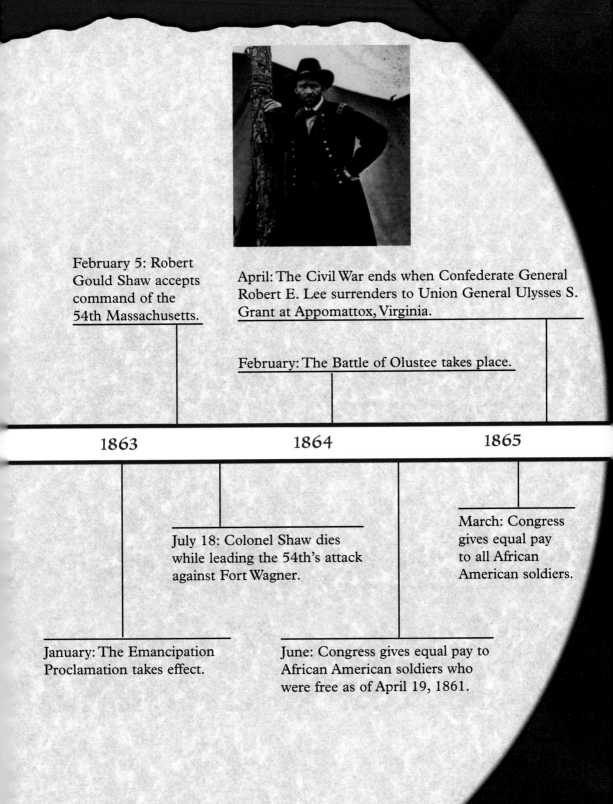

February 5: Robert Gould Shaw accepts command of the 54th Massachusetts.

April: The Civil War ends when Confederate General Robert E. Lee surrenders to Union General Ulysses S. Grant at Appomattox, Virginia.

February: The Battle of Olustee takes place.

1863   **1864**   **1865**

July 18: Colonel Shaw dies while leading the 54th's attack against Fort Wagner.

March: Congress gives equal pay to all African American soldiers.

January: The Emancipation Proclamation takes effect.

June: Congress gives equal pay to African American soldiers who were free as of April 19, 1861.

Glossary

abolitionist (ab-uh-LISH-uhn-ist)—a person who wanted to end, or abolish, slavery

bayonet (BAY-uh-net)—a long metal blade that can be attached to the end of a rifle

colonel (KUR-nuhl)—a military officer who usually is in charge of a regiment

compromise (KOM-pruh-mize)—the middle ground between two different ideas

Confederacy (kuhn-FED-ur-uh-see)—the nation formed by Southern states that seceded from the Union

contraband (KON-truh-band)—the goods that help a country or group fight a war; during the Civil War, slaves were referred to as contraband.

corps (KOR)—a large part of an army, which consists of many different smaller parts, including regiments

emancipate (e-MAN-si-pate)—to free a person or group of people from slavery

fugitive (FYOO-juh-tiv)—someone who is running from the law

infantry (IN-fun-tree)—soldiers who travel and fight on foot

regiment (REJ-uh-muhnt)—a group of up to 1,000 soldiers

secede (si-SEED)—to withdraw from a group or organization

For Further Reading

Blashfield, Jean F. *Abraham Lincoln.* Profiles of the Presidents. Minneapolis: Compass Point Books, 2002.

Burchard, Peter. *Frederick Douglass: For the Great Family of Man.* New York: Atheneum Books for Young Readers, 2003.

Clinton, Catherine. *The Black Soldier: 1492 to the Present.* Boston: Houghton Mifflin, 2000.

Graves, Kerry A. *The Civil War.* America Goes to War. Mankato, Minn.: Capstone Books, 2001.

Haskins, James. *Black, Blue, & Gray: African Americans in the Civil War.* New York: Simon & Schuster Books for Young Readers, 1998.

Stanchak, John. *Civil War.* Eyewitness Books. New York: Dorling Kindersley, 2000.

Places of Interest

Massachusetts Historical Society
1154 Boylston Street
Boston, MA 02215
http://www.masshist.org
This site holds many important U.S. historical documents.

Museum of Afro American History Boston
Administrative Office
14 Beacon Street
Suite 719
Boston, MA 02108
http://www.afroammuseum.org
This museum tells of the importance of African Americans to the history of the New England area.

National Park Service
Fort Sumter National Monument
1214 Middle Street
Sullivans Island, SC 29482
http://www.nps.gov/fosu
This park shows the importance of Fort Sumter and surrounding forts to the Civil War.

Robert Gould Shaw and 54th Regiment Memorial
Beacon and Park Streets
Boston Common
Boston, MA
http://www.nps.gov/boaf/site1.htm
This is the location of the memorial dedicated to Robert Shaw and the 54th Massachusetts.

Internet Sites

African American Civil War Memorial
http://www.afroamcivilwar.org/learn.html
Viewers can read facts about African American soldiers and sailors, the African American experience during the Civil War, the 1998 memorial, and the museum in Washington, D.C.

Battle of Olustee
http://extlab1.entnem.ufl.edu/olustee
This site contains information, photographs, and maps about the 54th Massachusetts at the Battle of Olustee in Florida in 1864.

National Park Service Civil War History
http://www.civilwar.nps.gov/cwss/history/aa_cw_parks.htm
This site describes many historic sites that preserve the history of African Americans in the Civil War.

Index